HUNT

hunt

poems

Jessica Cuello

WINNER OF THE 2016 WASHINGTON PRIZE

THE WORD WORKS
Washington, D.C.

FIRST EDITION

Cover Art: Matt Kish
Cover Design: Susan Pearce Design
Author Photograph: Gabriel Cuello

ISBN: 978-1-944585-07-5
LCCN: 2016957974

Acknowledgements

Blue Lyra Review: "The Whale Looks at Painted Depictions of Herself"

Corresponding Voices Anthology, Vol. 8: "The Castaway"; "The Right Whale's Head"

Hermeneutic Chaos: "The Dart"; "The Monkey-rope"

Menacing Hedge: "Ahab's Wife Senses His Brief Impulse Toward Home"; "The Chapel"; "The First Lowering"; "Skin, the Blanket"; "Squid"; "The Whale As a Dish"; "Tashtego Falls Into the Whale's Head"; "Not How the Whale Imagined His Touch"

Mud City Journal: "The Whiteness of the Whale"

Passages North: "Brit"

Prelude: "The Chase ~ First Day"

Prick of the Spindle: "The Carpet Bag"; "The Counterpane"; "Chowder"

RHINO: "Merry Christmas"

Thanks to the brilliant Caroline (Care-Care) Mann who helped me figure out the book's form.

Gratitude to Lesley Williamson and The Saltonstall Foundation for the time and space that allowed me to finish these poems.

Thanks to Joan Houlihan, Stephen Motika, and the 2015 Colrain Conference for giving me faith in the work.

Thank you to Matt Kish for the cover art. Thank you for being so generous.

And so much gratitude to Nancy White and the other judges of The Washington Prize. Thank you for believing in this work.

Contents

for Eduardo,
from the beginning

Loomings: The Wife at Home

Chapter 1

The body makes a sea:
a sea for mine, for the stay behind

When the men go
and ropes clatter at the dock

we hear them off, off
and inside my tumbling sea

a beast rolls over
on the clay bottom

I sense her lovesick eye
in the corner

cordoned on all sides
her beasty eye

where the rage pools
in the umbilical silt and moon

I subdue her trance
and claw, her dreamy eye

shrill with disappointment
and left to survive

The Carpet Bag

Chapter 2

He moves at night
like a candle
in a tomb. Free

to stumble,
a sudden disturbance
at the church's door:

an explorer.
We keep inside—
our bodies cannot move

alone on streets or boats.
It's unseemly.
We were born to keep

in walls and if we dream
of space, we must
be falling. Our limbs

move by task not will.
We were born in bed—
to imitate, hands made

to clench. We bring water.
Then silence, a baby.
We rock and feed,

tethered to our fathers,
to the others.
We never wander.

The Counterpane

Chapter 4

Not his real mother, I beat him
supperless
and shut him in alone,

found him up the chimney leaving
because he saw the chimney sweep
climb through and out.

Trying to contain the sudden flinch
and little bruise, I beat.
I beat to bring on silences.

I'm not good enough—
their tiny voices like a leak,
a speaking floor that won't shut up,
a no that says yes.

They're not your own
with eyes from elsewhere
and a mind, a whine, trying

to get down from the attic room,
trying to get free:
No one is.

Take the medicine,
sit down, learn the walls,
the way your arm

ends and the quilt begins—
where you end and the terror
visits—we live with it.

The Chapel

Chapter 7

they wear the trappings

grief encased and sewn

don't touch or enter

wear it cover the limbs

in the water his body

stares up from the bottom

how he sees the sky

through a layer of water

a fog that's how we know God

through a penned cloud

and the air is outside

or the body has not fallen

and the widows pick

if they will grieve or not

they have no news

no body

Chowder

Chapter 15

Leave the iron down with me.

Housekeeping and sexless,
I find the unmade bed, the tooth left.
I do not stop to feel. I feed the men.
Chop clams. Think I don't know
I'm the laugh and lackey?
Think I don't—

I carry bowls, I nag, begin. Alone
I undress my body—this dark home—
heavy, fish-smelling.
I set my necklace of polished
fish vertebrae on the dresser
and remember Mother's dry
arthritic hands that served
when they couldn't bend.

Leave the iron down with me.

I'm stopping death.
I found a body pierced
with a harpoon—an accident.
I'm making soup.
Thankless stirring,
the leftover of woman.

Merry Christmas

Chapter 22

sweet fields of your chest and cheek
sweet fields

the days until I see you eat
wrist bending to the plate

the days from Christmas until
next Christmas

days until the hull is oil-full
and turning home

the cordage rings
and you set sail

don't leave, don't leave
which I never said

which was need, come from the well:
the wishing well, the waiting well

a seed expanded in me
as I watched you eat, first mate

sweet fields of the table
and your face

isolated star, an inn
we begin

sailing into a season
spring is in store

spring is yet to be uncovered
meet my eye

though your face is far afield
though your face is a frame I tender

our glance is straw, newborn

Ahab's Wife Thinks of Her Honeymoon

Chapter 28

The house had hunter eyes
where the deathwish went.
Undress me in the yard.
Behind a bush.
I would die inside.
He calls me girl—resigned
and sweet. That girl repeats five times
whatever she will say.
She looks the other way
out of her life
when he throws her to the floor,
limp rag, a body with its holes.
A brute can be a good guy,
can provide.

Prayers Dissolve in Water.
Please Go, Says the Whale

Chapter 29

I heard a man pray
for another man.

I heard my bone
fasten to his body. His body

made like God. With a piece of me.
My likeness swallowed

as a crutch, a falsehood—leg.
Clump clump. It can't be no.
What of the limbs that walk
on flesh, then whale tooth peg.

What of how you saw me?
Great gulf. Blank, blank.
What inattentiveness is hate.

I don't dare dismantle prayer.
Our Father. Our broken body.
Our Lord. Lord of the seas,
do not darken me with
words and ink and incantation.
Please don't think of me.

Queen Mab: The Whale Has a Dream

Chapter 31

She hath been with me:

my tooth lodged in his leg
swimming through cold spots
where the sun was not
the water black

sleeping   my hand hit your chest
and the blanket bled

your eyes in my eyes and arms
in arms. I beat
you down   and beat against
the door. I swam, was flying,
was breach. And dove.
Fear was dust. Chase was over, old
and tired. Turned around. Turned face.
Turned rage and strength.
I left water. I grew legs.
I made a raft for the child,
but the men I sank.

Cetology

Chapter 32

List me as your animal.
Your pleasure, bound.

Make me in your names.
Nails. Voice. The brain in half.

An exhibition. Your list.
Your list to hunt and hype.

Write of me. To be
written means I have lives

and they are numerous.
All of us are black within.

Blackness is the rule
of organs and the brain.

Blackness is where we speed
and seek. Where you can't go.

Once we surfaced
and you observed a shape,

a mood, an angular fin,
wrinkled lips, oil like a porpoise.

Once we were on display.
Once we let you see

our eye, free and blinking
on the sea.

The Whale Hears Ahab's Explanation

Chapter 36

Beauty is a pasteboard mask

you claim, talk of the face

Strike through the mask

mask: skin, sinew, hump, and eye
below the mask: is I, is I

That inscrutable thing is what I hate

it is not a mask: I wear these hands
objects: nose, my crooked jaw

my objects oh me, my life
and object, take me, punch through

my property, take the thought
I swim inside this mask

I think there
Is my inheritance, is patient

is an ear, take binds
Take never open up, with all broken

take lance and never open
Beauty has no mind she has no mask

You hate because you think
to see is strike, to look beneath

to pierce and see below
You think to break

will open

Sunset

Chapter 37

He talks to no one there
To what can't swerve him

He says his course is iron rails
He says the lovely light
Does not light him

He says he wants
To dismember her

Underwater she releases air
She releases *click click click*
Words for prey and predator

He says his iron crown
Beats on his brain
Possession is his iron blood

Sad with power
He explains to no one there

His voice is a boom
He says he'd strike the sun
If it insulted him

He says *If she speaks
about the past he can't listen*

*That was long ago
and she was too emotional*

He must crush her will
Though it flailed and bled

Though it surprised
Like a hot metal fissure
In a stone

Pip, the Cabin Boy:
Forecastle at Midnight

Chapter 40

Who has fear now? White squall
white shiver, other men go,

but Pip stays and hangs on tight.
He saw them dance,

half a leg, half a face,
the sprawl and response of body.

They don't fear enough,
don't tremble, not born

into fear. Fear is the god in the dark,
white looming. He remains a boy

for them, a hoop for song.
They say the waves are women

but the sea is his skin
breaking, his skin is in

the whirling woods,
as rough

as it is immediate,
smack in the thick of it.

He is last on the forecastle,
aware of how alone his grip.

The Whale Reflects on Being a Hunted Object

Chapter 41

Rumors went that I had a taste
for blood. Piled upon my hump
was the hatred of a man.
How dare I stay alive?
I was meant to lie still
and let the point find me.
Meant to be the quietly violated.
The oil in my skull is sweet and old.
I won. I won. Little clicks of mouth,
like tapping in a tree.
This is peace. In my throat
when I sleep.
At the end I can finally explain
that I was afraid.

The Whiteness of the Whale

Chapter 42

Your enemy.
Stare. You made out

my body in the dark,
dumb and glowing—

a churchyard of snow.
A December field
but for the pink tongue

and prickly shadows. It was a shock.
A phantom, nothing to discern.

A giant blank. You used the eyes
of others to watch

for my body, strange
and shivering. Painted on top,

dressed with skin.
The paint was a lie
but the act of painting was real.

You stood on the abyss.
My body dove. It was speckled,

brown, earth-bound. The whiteness
was your own mind looking on.

The Whale Imagines Ahab Charting a Path

Chapter 44

A graphite
line runs through his skull
and teeth

His eye is pasted to my neck

My mottled body
in his head, my forehead white
beneath the dusk

I always wanted a picture of myself:
a pulse, a tethered eye

I always wanted a man who knew my mind

Too bad the graphite digs
too hard a path

and nothing's behind the teeth
but teeth

The First Lowering

Chapter 48

Lowered above my flesh strings,
harp of my mouth,
those who look for me
will find I shrink
because I was born
with a warning.
I was born with the tale
of Bluebeard's wives.
My mother told me that in the real world
one man carved rape onto
his victim's back.
Before I knew what real was.

The Hunted Whale Addresses the Starving Men

Chapter 52

Below the ship skeleton, the red rust
masts like beast skins,

below that weary,
below that despair,
the dropping trumpet
and the hunted.
Below the tired ship, the scrap,
the make believe trouble.

Below the chase you gave,
whoever died or starved
in your race, below

the helm, the sadness,
disappointment.

Below the trumpet, letters
addressed to Ocean,

below was my oil rolling in me.
Oil, skin, bones.

I was the animal:
cause of your grief
and hunger.
     Cause, oil, silent body
     below the ship.
     What you've done
     to me you've done to you.

Storytelling Overheard

Chapter 54

in sleep, rough tongue and gorged,
the story is told

for so long I say *Not It*, not playing,
just a landscape in the telling—

how can that be?

I'm the *raison d'être*:
I startle and straighten your back,

your eyes travel the road
of my skin, tilt at the throat

and all this time, you've gazed
into the sea at yourself

like you're trying on my broken jaw
but I am fighting for my life,

and I am the plot,
not the scenery—

The Whale Looks at Painted Depictions of Herself

Chapter 55

I opened to a page and saw my face
my legs, my backside
My skin was paper, two-dimensional

I recognized the printed torso first,
before my own, which was underwater,
a room unlit, a room I never entered

Mirrors in the sea are iridescent
mirrors in the sea are other creatures
waving back silk arms, beckoning

They have pictures of me,
none of them right
I am the brain with two eyes

I am not a brain to stop burning
It formed inside my mother
and burst out, my cells multiplied

To dive is to capture light, paint me
down there on the ocean floor,
or paint my nursing eyes, retracted

What is a face? My eyes have focal length
They see your trajectory at sea, dotted lines
that crisscross like a lie

I never wore that color or lifted my teeth wide
I never went back and tore that rope
I never swallowed those men

They drew me bursting out of waves,
they watched me from the sidelines
I left my body and entered their eyes

and looked back at my flank
and looked back at the places
where the tools would probe,

the outline, the nipples for feeding,
the endometrium absorbed
I thought it was another just like me

circling in the water
pounding her tail for home
I didn't burn their paper,

I looked for her, my lost mother
What is reflection?
I cannot live outside of water

Scrimshaw: the Whale Tooth Speaks

Chapter 57

Jackknife on extracted tooth,
dentist wand of pointed silver.
He carves a reverie onto me:
delicate outlines of men-o-war.

He races them around the poles,
moves them with each tiny cut.
He's anxious with his solitude. It beats
into his ear, the burn and crackle of the sun.

How did he get here? To the space of hopes,
space of indifference, to the
flecked tooth cramped with sky.

He frames me, captured in his mind.
Lonely whaler, carve a line. Curve waves
in my wake. Place black stars above my head.

Brit

Chapter 58

He thought the sea was his
to disturb and disturb.

My whale mouth swam open,
naked through vast yellow fields.
My appetite made swathes of blue.

In my cannibal sea, we eat our own
and we get eaten.

I thought reaching for one another
we reached the same land—
water aside, waves trembling.
I thought rest. Rest and devour,
quiet as rocks.

You heard the murmur of the fields;
you quivered in your skin.
You said, *Get dressed.*
I thought how sad men were
stepping with legs
into their pants.

I thought how sad men were,
vulnerable in their heads,

amassing
what they couldn't eat.

Squid

Chapter 59

My food rose in white ghost glory,
sent silence over the water,
came from an under
where forests begin and mountains.
What does my food remind you of?
How large the ground below desire—
when I dive I'm not of you. I seek
the sweet silk, headless. But to survive.
To be alive. And the pleasure is
that bite. The skin, the juice that runs.
Disgorge an arm, pulpy mass, cream.
Undulating apparition. Yes, I eat and tear.
Life unto life. Food unto food.
You are different: kill and sell.

The Dart

Chapter 62

And who knows how hard it is
to aim a dart? To keep it fixed.
To handle a male body. Only men know.
She could hear him from the basement
of the sea. How stiff
he lay wanting his fill of her.
He resented cross-purposes.
Her purpose at all.

How hard is it to follow
when the dart affixes?
To follow iron. Two-flue iron,
single-flue iron, toggle iron.
Wood to blackskin.
Tension in the rope.
If she had one path,
now she had another.

Go to sleep, she'd say, *I can hear
you thinking*. And he could feel her
leaving while she slept,
escaping him like water
and his neck had a crick
angled toward her.

The Whale As a Dish

Chapter 65

I am not alive anymore.
I have my parts:
the meat
the brain
the cream

I fed my baby
from the inside
out. And now
I am in the mouth
of a man; he holds
his little knife.

He stabs to eat.
I understand
hunger, the plunge
to stop the cramp,
raw beak,

yet sometimes
one eye meets
another and agrees:
not this flesh

not this blood
to oil the mouth.

The Shark Massacre

Chapter 66

They bite with dead mouths.
They bite their own
disembowelments.

Spin, snap.
They bite their own
and they bite after.

Lanterns lower on a massacre
in the water, the dark,
and off to the side.

Light makes color, color is not alive.
Color's not real.
Sharks are pale like human skulls,

no blush or blossom,
no neck to tuck a body in, no arm
to oversee a burial.

Crush the crepe flowers.
Bring on the hunger.
There was blood in the water,

a carcass, a group
with no faces, an absence
of miracle.

Skin, the Blanket

Chapter 68

Skin is the travelling body.
Press it where the feeling is.
It traffics in the world,

does not belong to itself,
belong to a hand on deck,
hand in the crowd,

hand out
inviting touch
outside itself.

It's up for grabs,
sheds the thinnest replicas,
dead cells and hieroglyphs.

Though I have none—
no wrists—unwound
like a spool and a rake,

exposed like a shoal,
I brought to it,
loved with it,

but was not the layers,
nor even the indecipherable
letters.

Her Decapitated Head, His Sphinx

Chapter 70

A head without a syllable. It's been
with horses drowned and sea moss:

weed tongue—the face that doesn't say,
the bodies overboard. The language dead.

Does the head hum? That sound isn't her.
That's wind in the chains.

Are there words in there? No—
just pictures of the sea: black and red and blue.

Color is pressed against her lids.
Her lips are lidded over the mouth

that sees like a ravine: people herded, dropped.
It's not a riddle. It's simple witness.

After he severs it, the captain asks the head
to speak, reveal—

The Monkey Rope

Chapter 72

Brothers dangle over me—two twins
bonded by my body

one holds the rope
that fastens to the other's belt
he dances on my back in socks

if one falls the other falls
he is his brother
his slippery foothold is his life

beautiful sacrifice and fraternity
I'm submerged
with my death and bitten flesh

waiting for his hook to lodge

The Right Whale's Head Speaks

Chapter 75

O Captor, my captor,
I'm fastened to the boat

and hands dive in my satin mouth.
The cutting-in. I am two parts.

My body over there.
My head a sulking sphinx,

a shoe-shape, an obedient.
Pour me out

to light, to burn,
to flicker in a human

eye. Animal blink,
the quiet code. I give

the riddled answer
of a thing. The wind

vibrates the blinds
that line my mouth: a hundred

bones with fringe
and useless now.

Tashtego Falls into the Whale's Head

Chapter 78

I encased Tashtego in
the numbness of my walls:
my loose dismembered head.
I was Dead by then—

still making life
with him upside-down
and fetal against me.
He fell and sank,

in complete darkness,
in an oily curtain
and the weight of a body in water
is the weight of water.

He would have slept for good
but Queequeg delivered him
by his hair, wiped my honey
from his face.

Brother wants brother
to breathe. I won't lie:
I made him spent in me.
We sweetened each other.

Not How the Whale Imagined His Touch

Chapter 80

What did this mean? That I was
beautiful? Your fingers

on my crevices of brain—
a kind of phrenology

down through my spine.
Where I pooled desire,

where I pooled memory:
the lapping water, your face.

Your face—so strange.
I'd nudged the boat, amazed

that you lived with objects
and walked on water—

that moment when I first
was sighted, when I waited

for you to leave,
for the boat to exit,

and instead your thumb
pressed against my teeth.

The Old Whale Is Captured

Chapter 81

I beat my one fin as fast
as old and blind will go

Where I had eyes, bulbs
have grown

They rope me three ways
I writhe to remove the barbs, but can't

I roll in blood to light their halls
What is light?

Flesh has grown over their instruments:
corroded harpoon, a lance head of stone:
metals inside me

They touch my yellow sore
I turn over like a waning world

I am my own death cabinet

The Fountain: How the Whale Hides

Chapter 85

for an hour or more without drawing
a breath

for an hour or more below the surface

a waiting black spot in thick water:
a mammal

breathe only in the arctic

breathe only when the light is gone

breathe only when his face recedes
his ship backtracks its invisible line

if you don't breathe you can't be
found

if you don't breathe you won't feel

if you don't breathe the hand passes
the skin stays clean, not pierced

if you don't breathe the remora
keep swimming, the harpoon
rests, the rope stays coiled

if you don't breathe, no fountain
no spray, no vapor

no *Thar she blows*
no stinging

once, I approached
once, curious
once, open like a lily
once, before you ruined
everything:

we're all tired
of your marauding

The Whale As Object of Desire

Chapter 86

I taught him to watch my beauty
with his forward eye. Tail, back,
behind, but never face, never
collected. An intact sideshow:

sightings of my plum-stone skin.
He wanted to catch me, tail
like wings. My side eyes saw
his tilted head, one-legged pants.

They saw it all, and dove.
Beauty has a thousand homes:
submission, absence, sweeping

sea. He wanted to have the last say
and wanting owes him nothing.

The Grand Armada

Chapter 87

on the outer circle kill all you can
wing them, so they can be killed later at leisure

at the center was the warm breath
eyes that gazed away from the breast
rich milk   not a fleet
skin still crumpled from the womb
new and delicate

the umbilical cord swayed
between a mother and calf
like a coiled jump rope

the calf nosed the boat
born and gentle
as a dog

the crew didn't ask for this scene
when they wrote their names
in the ship's registry and earned
a lay of 1/350th, no wages

it lifted them to sweet fields
to a home, stopped their minds
they thought of milk—heavy, sweet

on the outer circle
the cutting-spade kept cutting
the infant eyes were unaccusing

Girls As Schools of Fish

Chapter 88

Girls kneel by
their school desks
one behind the other
cover their heads
with crossed hands
to practice for holocausts
girls pull her wet arm
to the pool edge
right before she goes under
say *I will braid your hair*
looking back at the house fire
and the burnt arm
playing dead
on the neighbor's floor

Girls with their arms
as armor on the bus
at the store entrance
decide not to enter
take the long way
to avoid the house
the dark hall
parking lot
the older brother
ready to jump into
the road, jump out
of the window
counting heads
holding open the subway
door, and her and her and her
and her, *please eat* she says

Girls keep each other
as wards
to ready for fear:
to be overpowered
to be alone
when the shapes
at the edge of the field
agitate
and if one of them
is dragged aboard
or netted in the limbs
the rest swim nearby
smelling her blood
frantic for her body
to enclose her
in their own school

Rules for Being Captured, Rules for Being Owned

Chapter 89

Not a waif—always a home
elsewhere for the uprooted and chased—

line cuts into the neck, trails behind,
the rusty barbs

Possession is the law

Begin here. Leave off there.
Footsoles on a spot of earth—
to be caught
to be not
in possession
of the wrist bent below the head,
lips, hair what is in me
that waits, won't wait,
walks, swims, runs, and breathes
afraid   *Possession is the law*

Landlord to my thighs and neck.
Broker to my bone.

Lodged in the face,
dragging behind a rope.

Law lifts seaweed toward the sun,
moves out the tide, fills in the moon.
Law drops the rain.

Nerves begin at the end of my rope
the metal poke, the numb.

You don't know what you feel
what limb is yours
what weight you drag

you don't know if you love
a son daughter mother

Touch what belongs to another—
touch what belongs to yourself

touch the arm with the mouth
with the wrist touch the calf

skin possessed: wrapped in cords
and flying inside the head

Ambergris

Chapter 92

His desire pins a strange eye,
takes measure of my inside.
I am oblivious to this resin,
to this mine—a perfume

hardened in my bowels,
to take when I am dead, to take
secretions of the throat.
My guts are lined with spine and beak.

Labor makes it sweet.
I can't see the whole he sees.
He's seen the veins, the skin, the grey.

Does he grope for this rock
that I carry like an organ—
an afterthought—that I do not even carry.

The Castaway

Chapter 93

The sea keeps his body up
and his mind
spills a liquid way
into the dark
and his face with the blue
where the earth falls off
where God is not—only faceless
angels slither, gilled.

    Worth less than the whale lost

but born. To a mother, casket-dark.
He woke to who was there.
No one. Who was ripped
from him. A boy. Or who the sea.
Why must he invisible—
his feet turned white,
too white. Like sugar
in water, receding

    Worth less than the whale lost

but born and took up space.
A hand, pinprick.
Next, he.

Men Squeeze the Whale Flesh Together

Chapter 94

Across, diagonal,
separate from the hands,
behind, or at the edge.
What was. Nothing.
Light, dark. I squeeze
the spermaceti
and the oil runs.
When I grab a hand
by accident, call me Ishmael.
Later I may be another, love
another. But wait and see.
Fluid is the vat. Ahab is
always Ahab. He is he.
But I have touched
a hand and shifted,
smelled violets, lifted
my eyes, reached for grapes,
been recognized.
We are. We are something.
You make use
of every part of her
in the slaughterhouse
on deck,
cook and squeeze
her in a fraternal vat,
white-horse flesh,
tendons, muscle.
The sperm oil oozes
from globules, slides
across the hands

and we enter,
bloodied again,
into The Land of Nod.

The Try-Works

Chapter 96

forgetfulness of fire and I leap
into your face

will you hear me then?

redness and smoke
my red hell

burning with my own body
and your forgetfulness

Cook, fire the works

I saw you sweat

I saw you sleep and hallucinate
at the wheel

I saw you vulnerable
beside my burning skin

my left wing of smoke

my form you breathed
into your throat and nose

my single wing
red shape of fire

and even as you tilt
the wheel

capsize the boat
(almost)

you are not listening

The Doubloon

Chapter 99

Born in pangs
and shivered down
her legs

his pink unfolded
skin, vernix covered
like a coral pressed—

At 12 months
Ahab lost the mother
who shook him out

who named him
for a dead king
whose blood was licked

by dogs
a larger force—
the ticking of the womb

She mothered
his little monkey flesh
the powder of limbs, everyone

was a baby once
The gold nailed to the mast
is her, her womb

is a slave's wedding ring
grown into a tree
He sees, we see, they

see, I see, the gold
is the trinity, the twins
a tattoo on skin

each sees, each reads
his worth
here's the door

it's nailed
it's a mirror
you bring to it

The Forge

Chapter 113

Am I afraid of a man
or a metal bar?
Or a rope on a hook?

Or of my skin?
How soft my whole self:
like a snail turned over.

Or hammering, the red mass
of sparks,
the smoothing of the nails,

the spiky barbs? No, it's
the making itself,
the tools of hate I inspire.

A Whale Remembers
How Ahab Watched Her Die

Chapter 116

You blame the sun for setting

blame me that I bit
to save my life, that I refused
a cage

I turned slowly in the water
turning toward the sun to die

Nothing was missing before I bled
then I went missing everywhere
a series of rooms pieced together

North Pole and imaginary lines

I kept turning, turning
misplaced syllables, gargle sounds

You refused to accept the sun's exit
sent back the grief answer

waited for my body to roll face down at last
as if that meant

that you had won

The Whale-Watch

Chapter 117

By my side in the blackness
the men in the boat become watchmen.
Who made them so?
They don't sing.

Who made the body to hang,
to rise with gases, attached,
while my sisters echo sounds
and hold their breath?

I won't become a whale fall,
sunk and skeletal on the floor.
Half in water like a pail,
the ocean turned to shallow ditch.

Who sleeps beside my deadness,
my wet altar?
Who nods over this market worth,
my harvest?

The Log and Line

Chapter 125

Sir, I mistrust it; this lie looks far gone

Pip came up to the men
as if he were the lost line
being pulled back in
or the wood gone in the current
let go
no telling how fast the ship goes now
or where she is
no reflection in his eyes
not there—astern
he was lost with the line
cut off no more alive
no more inside
the self—like Ahab
who turned to Pip
for what had emptied out of him
the human part keeps reaching out

Pip touched Ahab's hand
called it velvet shark-skin

hand in hand
boy and man

torturers have children
and the devil loves

The Sailors Mistake the Seals' Cries for Dead Men

Chapter 128

The seals with their human faces,
the black-rimmed eyes ask, *Do you hear?*

One man fell from the mast
a splash, silent,
with years between the man
and mother. The buoy was thrown
and no hand reached up.

No wail so far from the womb.
Our life is not our life.
Our life is hers. We breathe
with her

her arm her neck her chest
the ripped out godhead
the self past the self
why apart alone on the shore
water between us, sea
between us. And the cry
the men insist is sailors dead,
is mermaids, is anything but this
where they begin
where they spear themselves.
Their own gloomy cry. Where did
I forget that I was I. Was I my.
Was I the cry that she made, cry
that joined two. That there are not two
no flesh apart. Forgot.

The Captain of the *Rachel* Begs Ahab for Help

Chapter 132

Do to me as you would have me do to you
you too have a boy

you too see his face in the dark
before you sleep and cringe
for his safety—and whisper, beg
for the others, whoever they are
to keep him

help him since he's broken from you always
once he walks
once the world
and once the sea

I scan for each dark spot.
He's 12. He's in a boat
adrift. Split the sea
with me and search. You must   must
my arms a gate, my eyes, my ship
my arms, my watch

son of my years
out there

your son is not my son my son
is not yours you are you
refuse you don't have a boy
a son there is a boy back home
with your name blood but you
don't belong to boys or sons
you forsake them

Ahab's Wife Feels
His Brief Impulse Toward Home

Chapter 132

I am in the house alone,
a child bride.

You take a breath
to see me for a second

in another eye. His wife
and family. *No,* you say,

No, no, no. No other way.
I can't undo

my narrative, give up
my limb. My limb is me.

My predator, you're loose.
I sing your name. Sing you away.

I stoop to gather lilies,
goldenseal. Flotsam for a man.

You're in the foreground,
I'm a child with a child.

Sound taps the hull
from underground and pulls away.

We married with no speech.
I tense for interruption

and wait my turn. A roar
is greater than a murmur.

I wait. I wait. I flinch
at thoughts of your return.

The Chase ~ First Day

Chapter 133

The word *brother* is not his word.
It's *Me and Them*. Alone too young
he set out to find
a flesh to press into his flesh,

went straight for a lover—direct—
tongue for tongue
and eyes for her. But everyone
turns enemy. *Crew* is utilitarian,

even her single hair on his tongue,
her naked skin, tastes hostile.
Still, in his first migration

he glanced behind
for brother eyes—for a godhead
figure he resembled.

Starbuck's Wife, Suddenly Awake

Chapter 134

waking from a dream
I went into the boy's room
touched my belly

touched my teeth
still in my mouth

your face in my face
your blue eyes you said

and I lay down
I didn't want to get up
the boy clung to my calf
like a sessile barnacle

because that was all I had:
the boy, Holy Ground
and nothing has changed

and you had hands once
we had a bed
now you're a ghost daddy

daddy of the sea my dream
I barely wished for this
to know

to make an end
to iron a seam and be wonderless
I had to kill hope

The Whale Is No Longer an Object of Desire

Chapter 135

I left him with his bloody patience
I left him with his splinters

I breathe through a spout,
Warm-blooded with a heart,
A chest he crushed with his,

A chest he roped to mine
And wet to death

Farewell to my arch
When I left him

Farewell to my underside
Unmarked

Farewell to my chase

Farewell to my object

His hunt was a kind of love:
catch the stranger and devour

How am I wild and he is not?

I was born from the buried place,
Born in a herd

He issued from the shore
The place grown upside down
He issued with his hurt saved up

He issued into exile, hurled,
He came, higher than the waves,
His lust an arsenal of instruments

Could it have been different?
He walked on water,
Laid hands on my leg, my calf:
Little muscle like a seal

One day I became pieces made,
A torn up species
I became my features

Then the conversations stopped
This is the one-sided part

About the Author

Jessica Cuello is also the author of *Pricking* (Tiger Bark Press 2016) and the chapbooks *My Father's Bargain* (2015), *By Fire* (2013), and *Curie* (2011). She has been awarded The New Letters Poetry Prize, a Saltonstall Fellowship, and The Decker Award from Hollins University for outstanding teaching. She teaches French in central New York.

About the Artist

Matt Kish is a self-taught artist and a librarian. He lives in Ohio with his wife, their frog, and far too many books. See more of his work at www.matt-kish.com

OTHER WORD WORKS BOOKS

Annik Adey-Babinski, *Okay Cool No Smoking Love Pony*
Karren L. Alenier, *Wandering on the Outside*
Karren L. Alenier, ed., *Whose Woods These Are*
Karren L. Alenier & Miles David Moore, eds.,
    Winners: A Retrospective of the Washington Prize
Christopher Bursk, ed., *Cool Fire*
Barbara Goldberg, *Berta Broadfoot and Pepin the Short*
Frannie Lindsay, *If Mercy*
Elaine Magarrell, *The Madness of Chefs*
Marilyn McCabe, *Glass Factory*
Ann Pelletier, *Letter That Never*
Ayaz Pirani, *Happy You Are Here*
W.T. Pfefferle, *My Coolest Shirt*
Jacklyn Potter, Dwaine Rieves, Gary Stein, eds.,
    Cabin Fever: Poets at Joaquin Miller's Cabin
Robert Sargent, *Aspects of a Southern Story*
    & *A Woman from Memphis*
Fritz Ward, *Tsunami Diorama*
Amber West, *Hen & God*
Nancy White, ed., *Word for Word*

THE TENTH GATE PRIZE

Jennifer Barber, *Works on Paper*, 2015
Roger Sedarat, *Haji as Puppet*, 2016
Lisa Sewell, *Impossible Object*, 2014

THE WASHINGTON PRIZE

Nathalie F. Anderson, *Following Fred Astaire*, 1998
Michael Atkinson, *One Hundred Children Waiting for a Train*, 2001
Molly Bashaw, *The Whole Field Still Moving Inside It*, 2013
Carrie Bennett, *biography of water*, 2004
Peter Blair, *Last Heat*, 1999
John Bradley, *Love-in-Idleness: The Poetry of Roberto Zingarello*, 1995, 2nd edition 2014
Christopher Bursk, *The Way Water Rubs Stone*, 1988
Richard Carr, *Ace*, 2008
Jamison Crabtree, *Rel[AM]ent*, 2014
Jessica Cuello, *Hunt*, 2016
B. K. Fischer, *St. Rage's Vault*, 2012
Linda Lee Harper, *Toward Desire*, 1995
Ann Rae Jonas, *A Diamond Is Hard But Not Tough*, 1997
Frannie Lindsay, *Mayweed*, 2009
Richard Lyons, *Fleur Carnivore*, 2005
Elaine Magarrell, *Blameless Lives*, 1991, 2nd edition 2016
Fred Marchant, *Tipping Point*, 1993, 2nd edition 2013
Ron Mohring, *Survivable World*, 2003
Barbara Moore, *Farewell to the Body*, 1990
Brad Richard, *Motion Studies*, 2010
Jay Rogoff, *The Cutoff*, 1994
Prartho Sereno, *Call from Paris*, 2007, 2nd edition 2013
Enid Shomer, *Stalking the Florida Panther*, 1987
John Surowiecki, *The Hat City After Men Stopped Wearing Hats*, 2006
Miles Waggener, *Phoenix Suites*, 2002
Charlotte Warren, *Gandhi's Lap*, 2000
Mike White, *How to Make a Bird with Two Hands*, 2011
Nancy White, *Sun, Moon, Salt*, 1992, 2nd edition 2010
George Young, *Spinoza's Mouse*, 1996

THE HILARY THAM CAPITAL COLLECTION

Nathalie Anderson, *Stain*
Mel Belin, *Flesh That Was Chrysalis*
Carrie Bennett, *The Land Is a Painted Thing*
Doris Brody, *Judging the Distance*
Sarah Browning, *Whiskey in the Garden of Eden*
Grace Cavalieri, *Pinecrest Rest Haven*
Cheryl Clarke, *By My Precise Haircut*
Christopher Conlon, *Gilbert and Garbo in Love*
    & *Mary Falls: Requiem for Mrs. Surratt*
Donna Denizé, *Broken like Job*
W. Perry Epes, *Nothing Happened*
David Eye, *Seed*
Bernadette Geyer, *The Scabbard of Her Throat*
Barbara G. S. Hagerty, *Twinzilla*
James Hopkins, *Eight Pale Women*
Brandon Johnson, *Love's Skin*
Marilyn McCabe, *Perpetual Motion*
Judith McCombs, *The Habit of Fire*
James McEwen, *Snake Country*
Miles David Moore, *The Bears of Paris*
    & *Rollercoaster*
Kathi Morrison-Taylor, *By the Nest*
Tera Vale Ragan, *Reading the Ground*
Michael Shaffner, *The Good Opinion of Squirrels*
Maria Terrone, *The Bodies We Were Loaned*
Hilary Tham, *Bad Names for Women*
    & *Counting*
Barbara Louise Ungar, *Charlotte Brontë, You Ruined My Life*
    & *Immortal Medusa*
Jonathan Vaile, *Blue Cowboy*
Rosemary Winslow, *Green Bodies*
Michele Wolf, *Immersion*
Joe Zealberg, *Covalence*

INTERNATIONAL EDITIONS

Kajal Ahmad (Alana Marie Levinson-LaBrosse, Mewan Nahro Said
Sofi, and Darya Abdul-Karim Ali Najin, trans., with Barbara
Goldberg), *Handful of Salt*
Keyne Cheshire (trans.), *Murder at Jagged Rock: A Tragedy by Sophocles*
Jean Cocteau (Mary-Sherman Willis, trans.), *Grace Notes*
Yoko Danno & James C. Hopkins, *The Blue Door*
Moshe Dor, Barbara Goldberg, Giora Leshem, eds., *The Stones
Remember: Native Israeli Poets*
Moshe Dor (Barbara Goldberg, trans.), *Scorched by the Sun*
Lee Sang (Myong-Hee Kim, trans.), *Crow's Eye View: The Infamy
of Lee Sang, Korean Poet*
Vladimir Levchev (Henry Taylor, trans.), *Black Book of the
Endangered Species*

CPSIA information can be obtained
at www.ICGtesting.com
Printed in the USA
FFOW02n1622230217
32769FF